Dealing With
Bad In-Laws

Dealing With Bad In-Laws

A Bible Study on Jacob and Laban

Sermon In A Book Series
Volume 2

First Edition

Copyright ©2017 Ken McDonald
All rights reserved

ISBN: 978-0-9798844-7-4

All Rights Reserved. No part of this publication may be reproduced, stored in a retrieval system, or transmitted in any form by any means, electronic, mechanical, photocopy, recording, or otherwise, without the prior written permission of the pubisher, except for brief quotations in critical reviews or articles.

All Scripture quotations are quoted from the Authorized Version of 1611

Designed by Ken and Terri Lee McDonald
Cover Photo: Shutterstock.com

www.everywordpublishing

Table of Contents

Preface...9

Introduction.......................................15

1. Personal Gain...............................41

2. No Respect...................................51

3. Can't Please Them........................63

4. Destroy Your Marriage..................71

5. Solution is Distance......................81

6. Hurting In-Law.............................91

7. Salvation......................................99

Preface

The stories in this book are true stories based upon personal experience as well as stories told me by others. I have changed names and particulars to protect their privacy.

As I cover the topic of in-laws I will be doing so, not from what I think, but from the standpoint of what the word of God says. As with all writers there will be unintentional human subjectiveness injected into the narrative. Therefore it is up to you the reader to study and check these things out in the Word of God. If you do not have the word of God, then you have a bad problem because my word is as good as yours, or should I say as bad as yours! The Bible states: ...yea, let God be true, but every man a liar. (Rom. 3:4)

When it comes to matters of controversy, (the

very nature of dealing with in-laws has to do with controversy,) there is a need for an authority that is far greater than the words of man, or the words of "Momma." The Word of God is that authority. When I say the Word of God I am referring to a book that I read daily which is the Authorized Version of 1611, also known as the King James Version of 1611.

There are many books available on the reason for accepting this Bible as the final authority, and if you do a google search you will find many. Yes, there will be those who detract from this position, but if you will study the facts, not opinions, you will find that the King James Version of 1611 has many facts about it that none of the other version can boast.

Let me give you one. There has never been one single error discovered in a King James Version of 1611 that will stand up in a court of law. In other words, there has never been a proven error found in a KJV 1611. What do I mean by that? While some will say a Greek or Hebrew word could be translated a "better" way, or a "more accurate" rendering, yet these are subjective statements. That is not what I am talking about. 2 Samuel 21:19 is an example of a mistake in many of the new versions.

> And there was again a battle in Gob with the Philistines, where Elhanan the son of Jaareoregim, a Bethlehemite, slew *the brother of* Goliath the Gittite, the staff of whose spear

was like a weaver's beam. (2 Samuel 21:19)

The King James 1611 reads *"the brother of."* By the way, 1 Chronicles 20:5 identifies the brother as Lahmi.

David slays Goliath, Gustave Dore' 1832-83

The New International Version, American Standard Version, Todays English Bible all exclude *"the brother of"* from 2 Samuel 21:19 making them in error, thus proclaiming a lie, and God cannot lie (Titus 1:2) and we know that no lie is of the truth. (1 John 2:21)

With "the brother of" removed then it reads:
>   1. ESV "...Jaare-oregim, the Bethlehemite, *struck down Goliath* the Gittite."
>   2. The NIV reads, "Elhanan son of Jaare-Oregim the Bethlehemite *killed Goliath* the Gittite."
>   3. The NASB reads, "Elhanan the son of Jaare-oregim the Bethlehemite *killed Goliath.*"

So I ask you, "Who killed Goliath?" Obviously David did:
>   1Sam. 17:49 And David put his hand in his bag, and took thence a stone, and slang *it*, and smote the Philistine in his forehead, that the stone sunk into his forehead; and he fell upon his face to the earth.
>
>   1Sam. 17:50 So David prevailed over the Philistine with a sling and with a stone, and smote the Philistine, and slew him; but *there was* no sword in the hand of David.

To say that Elhanan killed Goliath is a lie, which is what the new versions say. Titus 1:2

states that, "God cannot lie," therefore the new versions are not the word of God. This is merely one example but it illustrates my point.

Along with these facts there is over four hundred years of history that shows the effects, or "fruits" that result from people who adhere to the King James Version of 1611.

> 15 Beware of false prophets, which come to you in sheep's clothing...16 Ye shall know them by their fruits. (Matt. 7:15-16)

The modern versions have produced the fruits of liberal worldly and spiritually dirty Christianity that look, sound like and blend in with the world. Modern Christianity has lost its power and influence. It is now regarded with disdain and contempt, much the same way the Israelites abhorred the offering of the Lord due to the abuse of Hophni and Phinehas. (1 Sam. 2)

The fruits of the King James Version of 1611 can be clearly observed by the revivals and great awakenings of the 17th through early 20th centuries where jails emptied, bars were shut down, crime dropped so the police had very little to do, and marriages were restored and strengthened, not to mentioned the souls that were truly born again by the Spirit of God.

While far from exhaustive, my reasoning is based upon these few facts, as well as others not mentioned for the sake of space and time, that I am going to use this version as my final authority as I write this book.

Introduction

Bible text and story overview

Gen. 31:36 And Jacob was wroth, and chode with Laban: and Jacob answered and said to Laban, What *is* my trespass? what *is* my sin, that thou hast so hotly pursued after me? 37 Whereas thou hast searched all my stuff, what hast thou found of all thy household stuff? set *it* here before my brethren and thy brethren, that they may judge betwixt us both. 38 This twenty years *have* I been with thee; thy ewes and thy she goats have not cast their young, and the rams of thy flock have I not eaten. 39 That which was torn *of beasts* I brought not unto thee; I bare the loss of it; of my hand didst thou require it, **whether** stolen by day, or stolen by night. 40 *Thus* I was; in the day the drought consumed me, and the frost by night; and my sleep departed from mine eyes. 41 Thus have I been twenty years in thy house; I served thee fourteen years for thy two daughters, and six years for thy cattle: and thou hast changed my wages ten times. 42 Except the God of my father, the God of Abraham, and the fear of Isaac, had been with me, surely thou hadst sent me away now empty. God hath seen mine affliction and the labour of my hands, and rebuked *thee* yesternight. 43 And Laban answered and said unto Jacob, *These* daughters *are* my daughters, and *these* children *are* my children, and these cattle are my cattle, and all that thou seest is mine: and what can I do this day unto these my daughters, or unto their children which they have born? 44 Now therefore come thou, let us make a covenant, I and thou; and let it be for a witness between me and thee.

The trip had been sudden with no time to plan. His mother Rebekah feared for her son Jacob's life, and told him to flee. As he was quickly leaving the house his father stopped him, gave him some quick instructions, blessed him and sent him on his way. In the rush of it all many things were left behind as he was running for his life.

Introduction

What happened was Jacob had received the blessing from his father Isaac. Esau was furious at this. In those days your father's blessing meant that God would preserve and take care of you. It was a very valuable thing, but a few years earlier Esau, the first born son, came home from hunting very weary and hungry. Smelling the fresh pot of lentile soup that Jacob had just made, Esau said, *"Hey Jacob, give me some of that soup, I'm about to die from hunger!"* Jacob, having an eye for the spiritual replied, *"Sell me your birthright and I will give you some soup."* To which Easu replied, *"I'm about to die! What good is a birthright to a dead man? I swear before God, you can have my birthright. Now give me some soup."*

So Esau sold his birthright to Jacob for a bowl of lentile soup. Now, the reality of that foolish decision came to bear. The blessing was Jacob's, not Esau's, and Esau is contemplating ways to kill his younger brother Jacob. Rebekah realizes, *"...Behold, thy brother Esau, as touching thee, doth comfort himself, purposing to kill thee,"* and tells Jacob to flee.

In the panic and rush Jacob grabs next to nothing in the way of supplies for the journey. After walking all day and with the sun setting in the west he lays down and uses a stone for a pillow. Weary in body, and sad in spirit he falls asleep quickly. That night God appears to Jacob in a vivid dream. As the sun arose from the east

Jacob awoke, and with an astonished recollection he thought of the dream and what God had promised him in the dream. Talking to himself he says, "*Surely the Lord is in this place and I knew it not.*" He names the place Bethel which means house of God.

Journeying on eastward he finally comes to Ur of the Chaldees, which is the land of his mother. Stopping at a well just outside of town he sees people loitering around with flocks of sheep.

Walking up to the men Jacob asks: "*Hey, do you guys know a man by the name of Laban? He is the son of Nahor.*"

A very encouraging reply came back from them: "*Yeah, we know him, and look ye there, here comes Rachel his daughter. She's the purty one.*"

Jacob squinted, took a quick upward glance at the sun and said to himself, "*What is she doing coming to the well at this time of day? It's high noon.*" He then said to the men again, "*Are you guys going to water your sheep?*"

They replied, "*Not right now. We have to wait until all of the flocks arrive and then the stone has to be rolled away from the mouth of the well before we can water the sheep.*"

The trip had been long and Jacob was in no mood to wait another four hours for the stone to be rolled away. "*Little Lady,*" he said with a curious excited tone, "*You mind if I water the flock of sheep you brought?*" Surprised by his

Introduction

offer she replied, *"Uh, sure that would be great!"* Jacob went to the mouth of the well and rolled the stone away all by himself. He then watered all the flock of sheep that Rachel brought.

Jacobs' dream, Gustave Dore' 1832-83

19

After days of lonely travel through a wilderness as well as knowing no one along the way, here was family. A relative, a cousin of his and by the time he was done watering the flock he could contain his emotions no longer. With tears welling up in his eyes he reached out, hugged Rachel, kissed her on the cheek and wept on her shoulder.

Rachel wondered, *"What is wrong with this guy? I think he is crazy!"* But then she heard him say, *"I'm your cousin Jacob. I'm the son of Rebekah your aunt."*

Rachel replied with excitement, *"Oh! I've got to go tell Dad. Wait 'til they hear this."* And she took off for home like she had been shot out of a cannon, leaving Jacob there with the flock. Jacob wiped his eyes and looking up realized the men were staring at him. Not sure what to say, but having a heart full of joy he said to them, *"All is well,...all is well,"* and then to himself he said, *"Thank you, Lord,"* and let out a deep sigh of relief.

Jacob finely arrives at Laban's house and is welcomed like family, for he was family. After a month Laban asks him what he would like to work for in order to stay with them. To this Jacob replied, *"Well sir, Uh..."* About that time Rachel looked at him with a twinkle in her eye. Jacob seeing that then said to Laban, *"Sir, I would like to work seven years for you in order to marry Rachel."* Rachel blushed as joy filled her heart. Laban then replied, *"That's good! It is better that I give her to you than some other man. It's just hard to find a good man these days and I think that Jacob, you're a good man. I can think of no one better that I would like my daughter to be married to. Let's shake on it."*

The next seven years Jacob worked for Laban, his future father-in-law, and those years seemed like just a few days because he loved Rachel so much.

Finally his seven years were up, but Laban didn't say a thing about giving Rachel to Jacob to marry. Jacob recounted the time and sure enough it had been seven years, but Laban wasn't saying a thing. A bit perplexed about it he waited a few days but could contain himself no longer. Approaching Laban one day Jacob asked him, *"Sir? I'm not sure if you know but it has been seven years since we made our agreement that I would be given your daughter Rachel for marriage."*

A not too convincing expression of surprise came over Laban as he responded *"It has?"* To which Jacob, slightly frustrated, said, *"Yes, seven years were fulfilled two weeks ago. I was waiting for you to bring the subject up but it seemed like you forgot."*

Laban kind of hedged around his words trying to figure out what to say. He knew all along the time was up, but ever since Jacob had arrived the old farm began to turn a profit. If he married Rachel he would then leave and the profits might stop coming in for Laban knew that God was with Jacob, and that God was blessing the farm because Jacob was there. Laban didn't care about Jacob. He just wanted to use him to bring in the money.

Laban replied, "Ok...Oh yeah Jacob, well you are so right! Forgive me, forgive me, it just slipped my mind. Give me a couple days and we will put the marriage all together."

A couple days went by and it was time for the marriage. In those days marriage was much simpler. There was a party and then in the evening the father of the bride brought her to the tent where Jacob was. There were no lights, candles or flashlights. All was dark as Laban ushered Leah, Rachel's sister into the tent.

In the morning Jacob awoke. Turning on his side to behold his beautiful new bride he shuddered and with a loud expression said, "What? L...L...Leah! What are you doing here!" Leah replied, "My father told me to go into your tent instead of Rachel. I am now your wife."

Jacob flew out of the tent astonished, perplexed, and in a bit of anger. Finding Laban he came up to him face to face and said, "What have you done? Why did you give me Leah, when I worked for Rachel?" Laban cooly replied, "Because it is not the custom for the younger to be married before the older. Leah had to be married first."

Jacob replied, *"You never told me this. Why didn't you?"* To which Laban replied, *"Well, you never asked. But let's make another deal. You promise to work for me for another seven years and I will give you Rachel to wife."* *"You mean I have to wait another seven years before I can marry her?"* Jacob hotly replied. *"No, Jacob, you can have her in a week, but you must work for me for another seven years."* *"OK!"* Jacob replied, *"I'll work another seven for you."* But at the end of that week Jacob made sure he was married to Rachel for she was the one he loved.

In those next seven years many children were born to Jacob. Besides Rachel and Leah giving birth, they each had a maid into which Jacob went and had children by them as well. I don't have time here to explain it all but you can read the story yourself in Genesis chapter 30.

At the end of the seven years Jacob has a desire to get out of there. He was spending his days out in the fields, and sometimes for many days at a time, while his wives and children were staying in Grandpa Laban's house. As each month passed by Jacob began to feel more like an outsider than the husband and father of his children. Oh, they were always glad to see him when he came home, and they always gathered around him when he was home. But it seemed that his orders from Laban kept him more and more away from home.

Not only that but Laban kept changing his pay

and if any animals were lost, stolen, or eaten by wolves that came out of Jacob's pay check. The nights were cold and the frost lay upon him as he shivered under his bedroll. It was ok as long as the camp fire kept going, but once he fell asleep the fire only lasted a couple hours. Then the frost came in until the sun arose and warmed him and the earth around.

In the summer the days were long and hot. Water was sometimes scarce so Jacobs lips became dry and chapped. At times cracking and bleeding. Dust clung to his sweaty skin, then dried on his face like a covering of mud. It was hard work.

Many a long day, Jacob labored out in the fields with the cattle, but his mind often drifted back to his family. He missed them so, but what could he do? As he thought to himself, *"My father-in-law gave me the orders and work, so here I am."* His thoughts would turn into arguments within his breast. Then he would wrestle with the thought, *"How can I go against my father in law? After all, he has been good to me. He gave me a place to live, my wives, as well as a job."* But the more he wrestled with his situation the more he wanted out. It had been fourteen years and as far as Jacob was concerned it was time to leave.

After coming in from the field he walked right up to Laban and said, *"I have worked fourteen years for thy two daughters. You know how hard*

Introduction

I have worked for you and I think it is time for me to be going. Give me my wives and my children for I believe the Lord wants me to return to my home land."

Jacob felt kind of strange having to ask for his own wives and children, but that's how it was. Laban had control of everything, including Jacob's family. It was almost as if Jacob was an outsider. Laban acknowledged Jacob if he had to when Jacob was home, but other than that Laban did all he could to separate him from his family. In Laban's mind it was becoming more and more his family. It was only when Jacob came home that the stark reality bore into Laban's mind that the family was Jacob's not Laban's. So Laban did all he could to keep Jacob away.

Now, though, it had been fourteen years since the original agreement. Laban could not ignore that fact. Again his scheming, plotting, selfish mind raced seeking to find a way to keep his daughters and grandchildren home with him. The thought of losing them to Jacob and their moving away brought a furious anger upon Laban. With clenched fist and gritting his teethe he would say under his breath, *"I will NEVER let my family leave my home. There is only one man that stands in my way and his name is Jacob. That sniveling little son-in-law of mine, but I can handle him."*

Calmly, with a smooth manipulating tone in

his voice Laban said to Jacob, *"Jacob, Jacob, lets sit down and talk about this. Look, I know at times it may have been difficult for you, but look at how well your family is doing. They love it here for this is home. As a matter of fact they don't even want to leave. I also know that the Lord has blessed me since you arrived fourteen years ago. Tell me, what do you want? How can we make this right?"*

Jacob thought for a minute, *"I don't want to stay here another minute, but how am I going to take care of my family?"* He then replied, *"OK here is what I want. I don't want one thing from you, but I will go through the cattle and when any are born speckled, spotted or brown I will take those sheep. All of the others shall be thine."*

Laban laughed within himself, *"Boy, you are such a fool!"* He then replied, *"That is a deal!"*

Over the next six years God blessed Jacob in a marvelous way. The cattle began to bear speckled spotted and brown offspring. Thus in six years Laban's flocks had diminished to very small anemic flocks, while Jacob's flocks were multiplying as well as strong and healthy.

About that time Jacob, walking across the dusty bare dirt front yard, overheard some of Laban's sons talking. They were kind of huddled up at the side of the front yard and had not noticed Jacob as he walked past. They were talking intently, but as Jacob passed by he heard one of them with a jealous anger in his

Introduction

voice say, *"He's taken all that was our father's. He has our herds, flocks and everything else."* Jacob then stepped up onto the porch and Laban came out of the house with a kind of mean glare upon his face as he stared at Jacob. A very strong feeling that he was not welcome there came over Jacob. It was such like he had never experienced before and with it he realized it was time to leave.

The next day God spoke to Jacob and told him, *"Jacob, return to the land of thy fathers, and to thy kindred; and I will be with thee."*

With this light from God Jacob knew that it was time to go. He then called his wives and told them that it was time to leave, and that the whole family was going back to Canaan.

Rachel spoke up first and said, *"Dad doesn't have anything left here anyway."* Then Leah replied, *"That's for sure! There is nothing to stay for here."*

Jacob knew one thing for sure. This time he was not going to ask Laban for his wives. He was taking his wives and family together and he was not going to mention it at all to Laban. It was none of his business anyway. Inside though Jacob had a fear that Laban would kill him and take the family back by force. He knew at the least Laban might take the family and tell Jacob to go home. He then imagined Laban bellowing out, *"My daughters and my children are not going with you!"*

Dealing With Bad In-Laws

This thought would bring a prayer to the lips of Jacob, "Oh Father! Help and protect me and my family from Laban. Lord, I need your help." Then it would seem to comfort him as he was reminded by the Spirit, "God told you to go home. Everything will be alright."

The day came and Jacob set his children and his wives on camels. Then with his flocks of sheep, and all that he had they departed for the land of Canaan. Jacob knew that Laban would be busy shearing his few sheep which would give him more of a distance by the time Laban realized that he had left.

It took Laban three days to find out that Jacob had left. Upon hearing this Laban flew into a rage. Barking out orders he yelled for the servants, and all of his sons, "Get your weapons and gear. Jacob has stolen away in secret from us. He has taken my daughters, my children and we are going to bring them back." Then under his breath he muttered through grit teethe, "Jacob, your days are numbered." What Laban didn't realize was that Jacob had Esau's blessing and the value of that blessing was now going to be revealed.

The camels kicked up the dust as Laban and his sons rode out of the front yard in a dead run. Leaving the house to just a few servants Laban and the boys had Jacob on their mind and murder in their hearts. It took seven days to catch up with Jacob, but on the night of the fifth day God came to Laban in a dream and told him, *"Laban, if you say anything good or bad to Jacob I will kill you. Got it?"* Laban opened his eyes in fear and trembling. Then whispering in the dark he said, *"Yes Lord, I got it."*

The frustration level in Laban was now at an all time high. He could no longer, by force, take back what he believed was his. The weapons and man power he brought were now useless. God was helping Jacob.

On the seventh day Laban found Jacob camped in the mount of Gilead. The meeting did not go as Laban wanted it to, for Laban's hands were tied. God had made it so. Finally with frustration, tears, and sorrow mixed with anger Laban exclaims to Jacob, *"What can I do?"*

Laban had come to do some things to Jacob, but God stopped him. With frustration and sorrow Laban cries, *"These are my children, and these are my daughters, these are my cattle and all that I see here is mine, and what can I do?"* The only thing God let Laban do that day was to say good-bye to all of JACOB'S FAMILY.

You see, Laban was a bad in-law and there are a number of reasons why. Not only so, but the Bible gives you the solution in order to deal with a bad in-law. To make these solutions known from the pages of the scriptures is the purpose of this book.

Overview of Marriage

Marriage was instituted by God;

> Therefore shall a man leave his father and his mother, and shall cleave unto his wife: and they shall be one flesh. (Genesis 2:24)

Yet from that time until now it has been attacked and sought to be destroyed. As time goes on, and as this age of Christianity comes to an end, marriages are attacked more and more. It has wisely been said by preachers of old, *"As the home goes, so goes the country."*

The rate of divorce for married women, fifteen years of age and older, has well more than doubled since 1940. According to the U.S. Census Bureau in 2006 the ratio of marriages to divorce is 2 to 1. (Monthly Vital Statistics Report, Volume 43, No. 9, March 22, 1995, Centers for Disease control and prevention)

Lately though, the divorce rate is dropping due to the fact that people aren't even bothering to get married. Do you know what that makes the woman in such a situation? Biblically, it makes her a concubine.

Generally there are three main causes for divorce. The first and main cause, outside of pride (Only by pride cometh contention: Prov. 13:10), is money. Arguments arise about how to spend the money. One person takes more than they should and spends it on their self without taking the other into consideration creating resentment in the marriage. What is needed is the realization that you will be happiest when your desire is to make your spouse happy. You will reap what you sew, and you will always reap more than you sew. Before I was married a man gave me some good advice which was this; *"If there is only one apple left, and you both want it, then give it to her."*

I know of a couple that is now divorced. They did not have much money, yet she would stay on the phone with her mother and run up the bill, even though her husband had told her not to. When they moved out of the house they were renting I saw where the phone had been ripped off the wall. No doubt, frustration over the inconsiderate use and spending of what little money they had.

Another major cause of divorce is arguments over how to raise the children. When should they be spanked, or even if they should ever be spanked. How to discipline them. One spouse gets the kids on his or her side against the other spouse and it ends up a divided home. "...a house divided against itself falleth. (Luke 11: 17) That can cause divorce.

Another cause of divorce is in-laws. In-laws can create great havoc in a marriage, even to the point of destroying it. How does one biblically deal with a bad in-law? That is the subject of this book. Though a very serious subject, yet problems from in-laws are so common that there are many jokes about in-laws.

One day a young man was walking along a beach after having a fight with his mother in-law

Dealing With Bad In-Laws

who was back at the house. He and his wife lived in a small house not far from the ocean and his mother-in-law had come for a visit. It was a warm sunny day, and the breezes blew softly, the seagulls screeched as they flew over head, but he didn't notice. His head was looking downward as he griped to himself out of frustration. He kicked the sand as he walked along spraying up little brief clouds and then they would settle back down.

Then he kicked the sand again when with curiosity he spotted a bottle. It looked like a bottle he had seen in story books. Why, it looked like Aladdins' lamp. He picked it up and pulled the cork out of the end, and sure enough this big old green genie came out. His eyes grew big with amazement and then he heard the genie speak to him is a deep strong voice, "You have three wishes, but I must warn you, what ever you ask for, your mother-in-law gets double." He slowly and thoughtfully replied, "O.K."

"For my first wish I would like a million dollars." The Genie then replied, "Now you know that I will have to give your mother-in-law two million dollars."

He replied, "Yes, I know, but that's alright."

"For my second wish I would like a great big ten bedroom ten bath mansion." The Genie then replied again, "You know, I must give your mother-in-law a mansion twice as big."

He replied again, "Yes, I know, but that is

alright."

Then in the inspiration of the moment he asked for his third request. *"I would like some one to beat me half to death."*

Another one of the jokes goes like this:

He didn't want her to come along, but she insisted, so George's mother-in-law came with them on vacation. But during their vacation and while they were visiting Jerusalem, George's mother-in-law died.

With death certificate in hand, George went to the American Consulate Office to make arrangements to send the body back to the states for proper burial.

The Consul, after hearing of the death of the mother-in-law told George that the sending of a body back to the states for burial is very, very expensive. It could cost as much as $15,000.00.

The Consul continued, in most cases the person responsible for the remains normally decides to bury the body here. This would only cost $150.00.

George thinks for some time and answers, *"I don't care how much it will cost to send the body back; that's what I want to do."*

The Consul, after hearing this, says, *"You must have loved your mother-in-law very much considering the difference in price."*

"No, it's not that," says George. *"You see, I know of a case years ago of a person that was buried here in Jerusalem. On the third day he arose from*

Dealing With Bad In-Laws

the dead! I just can't take that chance."

The following one I've heard in various versions over the years.

A newlywed farmer and his wife were visited by her mother, who immediately demanded an inspection of the place. The farmer had genuinely tried to be friendly to his new mother-in-law, hoping that it could be a friendly, non-antagonistic relationship. All to no avail though, as she kept nagging them at every opportunity, demanding changes, offering unwanted advice, and generally making life unbearable to the farmer and his new bride.

While they were walking through the barn, during the forced inspection, the farmer's mule suddenly reared up and kicked the mother-in-law in the head, killing her instantly. It was a shock to all no matter their feelings toward her demanding ways.

At the funeral service a few days later, the farmer stood near the casket and greeted folks as they walked by. The pastor noticed that whenever a woman would whisper something to the farmer, he would nod his head yes and say something. Whenever a man walked by and whispered to the farmer, however, he would shake his head no, and mumble a reply.

Very curious as to this bizarre behavior, the pastor later asked the farmer what that was all about. The farmer replied, *"The women would say, 'What a terrible tragedy' and I would nod my head and say 'Yes, it was.' The men would then ask, 'Can I borrow that mule?' and I would shake my head and say, 'Can't, it's all booked up for a year.'"*

It's a curious thing though, that as I researched for jokes on in-laws it was interesting to note that I could not find any on father-in-laws. Surely there must be some, but the majority by far are the jokes about mother-in-laws.

Also in my research I found a web site titled, "Ihatemyinlaws.com". On this web site people write in and "vent" or tell about their experiences with in-laws. The language can be poor on this site. I also noticed that well over ninety five percent of the articles were written by women. I'm sure there must be some on the site written by men, but I did not read one.

As a preacher in the ministry for over twenty years, I have never heard a sermon on in-laws. I have heard passing remarks and recommendations of what to do if you have a bad in-law, but I have never heard a sermon entirely on the subject of a bad in-law. This seems odd to me since in-laws are one of the major causes of divorce, and are a major cause of trouble in a marriage.

One day my wife Terri, my daughter Rebekah, and I went out about town to get some errands done. We pulled up in front of a store, and I decided to stay in the truck, while they went in

Dealing With Bad In-Laws

and did some shopping.

Sitting out in the truck I decided to turn the radio on and see if there was anything worth listening to, so as to pass the time. Since there was no sports radio on, which if it gets raunchy I turn it off as well, and I don't care for most "Christian" radio, so I ended up with Dr. L_____, one of those call in and get counceling shows.

Though I was not all that excited about it, yet I thought that I would listen and see if I could get some sermon illustrations, and I did. I got this one that I am going to tell you about.

This newly married girl calls up Dr. L_____ and Says, *"Hi, Dr. L_____. I have a question for you."* (I will just tell you the story.)

Dr. L_____ I have been married for six months but I am thinking about leaving my husband, and I want to know what I should do. Dr. L_____ asks her if she loves him and she said that she did. She also said that he was a hard worker and loved her too. The problem was that her mom and dad had made her an offer that she could go to any school she wanted and they would give her a blank check for tuition and all the costs, but there was one catch. She had to divorce her husband. It was a tempting proposition to her and had put her in a quandary as to what to do.

Even Dr. L_____ seemed aghast at the story and proceeded to tell her that she had made a vow before God, and that she should stay with her husband and keep her vow before God. The young newlywed agreed, and it seemed plain that she wanted to stay with her husband, but her parents were putting pressure on her to leave him. Dr. L_____'s counsel was good counsel, though I would have added something. I would have told her to get away from her parents and if they persist in their attempt to destroy her marriage that she will have to cease all communication with them.

Those parents meant well, but they were contrary to the word of God. They were wrong in what they were trying to do. It was none of their business.

> Therefore shall a man leave his father and his mother, and shall cleave unto his wife: and they shall be one flesh. (Gen. 2:24)

The problem arises when the severance is not understood, nor accepted. What I mean by that is when you are married you have departed from your mother and father. They are no longer over you. Even Abraham, one of the great men of the Bible, had a problem with this in the word of God. Notice what is recorded:

> Now the LORD *had said* unto Abram, Get thee out of thy country, and from thy kindred, and from thy father's house, unto a land that I will shew thee. (Gen. 12:1)

Notice the *"had said"* is past tense.

Dealing With Bad In-Laws

The Lord tells Abraham to get out of the country, and leave your family there, but Abraham does not do this. He takes his father with him, as well as his nephew. This is not what the Lord told him to do. Abraham does not want to leave his family. Notice:

> And Terah took Abram his son, and Lot the son of Haran his son's son, and Sarai his daughter in law, his son Abram's wife; and they went forth with them from Ur of the Chaldees, to go into the land of Canaan; and they came unto Haran, and dwelt there. (Gen. 11:31)

Terah, Abram's father, hears what God told his son to do, and assumes control of the situation. Notice that *"Terah took Abram,"* and he also took Lot. Terah was not supposed to do that. Terah rebels against God, as well as causing his son to disobey the Lord as well. Then came he out of the land of the Chaldaeans, and dwelt in Charran: and from thence, when his father was dead, he removed him into this land, wherein ye now dwell. (Acts 7:4) The Lord ended up killing Terah and forced Abraham to get away from family. The remaining problem was that Lot was still with him. God did not want any family to go with Abraham.

If you know your Bible, or if you study it out, you will find that Abraham does not get blessed until he separates from Lot. Abraham had a hard time with getting away from family, and he is not the only one. The leaving of father and mother is still a hard task today, and many couples suffer because the severance is not properly performed nor understood by the husband and wife.

Sure, you may desire a big happy family. One where you all get along and actually enjoy being together. You might even believe that it is the way it ought to be, after all, it's family. Let's get together for the holidays, and we will trade off each year whose house we will meet at. If your family does that, then count your blessings. That is an ideal situation, but realize that you are in a great minority.

You may even be thinking that because your family is saved, then that is all the more reason that the family ought to be able to get along, and love each other. I do not mean to be cynical, but it probably will be worse for you, if you all are saved.

> 51 Suppose ye that I am come to give peace on earth? I tell you, Nay; but rather division: 52 For from henceforth there shall be five in one house divided, three against two, and two against three. 53 The father shall be divided against the son, and the son against the father; the mother against the daughter, and the daughter against the mother; the mother in law against her daughter in law, and the daughter in law against her mother in law. (Luke 12:51-53)

Dealing With Bad In-Laws

Now that is what the the Lord Jesus Christ said about it. If you are in a situation where you do not get along with your in laws then you must realize that you are scriptural. Or if you are married and do not get along with your own parents, then realize that you are scriptural. Notice the in-laws in the passage show that it is dealing with a marriage situation, not a son or daughter that is still living at home. This is not an alibi for a child to be rebellious to the father or mother.

You may have a Rodney King, (Circa Sacramento, CA early 90's), mentality and ask, *"Can't we all just get along?"* You ought to respect your in-laws, or your own family, and try to get along for it is the best way. But the answer to that question is likely to be, "No," you can't all get along. Do all you can, without going against Scripture, to get along with them, but after having done your best then you have scripture to support your decision. If you are having trouble with in-laws, the sooner you realize this the better. No, you are not backslidden, that is just the way it is.

1

Personal Gain

Gen. 31:38 This twenty years *have* I *been* with thee; thy ewes and thy she goats have not cast their young, and the rams of thy flock have I not eaten. 39 That which was torn *of beasts* I brought not unto thee; <u>I bare the loss of it; of my hand didst thou require it, whether stolen by day, or stolen by night.</u> (Emphasis added) 40 *Thus* I was; in the day the drought consumed me, and the frost by night; and my sleep departed from mine eyes. 41 Thus have I been twenty years in thy house; I served thee fourteen years for thy two daughters, and six years for thy cattle: and <u>thou hast changed my wages ten times.</u> (Emphasis Added) 42 Except the God of my father, the God of Abraham, and the fear of Isaac, had been with me, surely thou hadst sent me away now empty.

Gen. 30:26 Give *me* my wives and my children, for whom I have served thee, and let me go: for thou knowest my service which I have done thee. 27 And Laban said unto him, I pray thee, if I have found favour in thine eyes, *tarry: for* I have learned by experience that the LORD hath blessed me for thy sake. 28 And he said, Appoint me thy wages, and I will give it. 29 And he said unto him, Thou knowest how I have served thee, and how thy cattle was with me. 30 For *it was* little which thou hadst before I came, and it is now increased unto a multitude; and the LORD hath blessed thee since my coming: and now when shall I provide for mine own house also?

Why was Laban a bad in law? What did he do, or not do, that made him a bad in-law?

A bad in-law will use you for personal gain.

A bad in-law is one who will see you, not as a son or daughter-in-law, but as a dollar bill. The Bible says that, "The love of money is the root of all evil," (1 Tim. 6:10) and that love will rear its ugly head through in-laws quite often.

As a newly married couple or, even if it has been years, do not seek, nor allow support to come from family. You need to support yourself, and I am writing to you men, you husbands that are reading this. It is your responsibility to support your family. Maybe your support isn't of the level your wife desires, or that your in-laws desire, but it is still your responsibility as the head of your house to support your wife and children. They are looking to you for that support and leadership. That is the position that God put you in as the head of your home.

There are instances of accidents where the man is crippled and unable to provide this way. This is an exception and a difficult trial that God can give you grace to endure the hardness as a good soldier of Jesus Christ. For a real man, to not be able to provide for his family is worse than the malady of his body. But then there are men, I use the term loosely, who are lazy bums not worth feeding. "For even when we were with you, this we commanded you, that if any would not work, neither should he eat." (2 Thes. 3:10)

To the wife, if your husband is working and doing his best to provide for you then be thankful and support him. Pray for him. There are women who don't have a man who is even trying. Most of the stories of frustration on ihatemyinlaws.com are due to men living off of family instead of bearing up under their responsibility and providing for their own family.

Laban realized that he was getting blessed because of Jacob's presence, and because of it, he did not want to let Jacob go. It was not that he liked Jacob, it was that he was getting rich off of Jacob.

A bad in-law may even fight you if they see that they can not profit from you. There has been many a parent who has persuaded their son or daughter about who to marry all because of a dollar bill. A young girl comes to her mother and father and asks, "What do you think of Johnny?" Her parents then reply: "*Oh, honey, you don't want to marry Johnny. I know he is a nice boy, loves the Lord, and he seems to really care about you, but I don't think you will be happy if you marry him. You ought to try for Sammy. He's a real nice boy and so smart, plus his dad is rich and you will be well off for the rest of your life.*" And in the back of their mind they are thinking, "*and you will be able to take care of us when we get old.*"

Many a parent child marriage conference has gone like that. You had better remember that money won't make a happy marriage. It takes a true love for each other, the Lord, and a walk with the Lord on both husband and wife's parts to make a happy marriage. I remember hearing someone say a good marriage is where both husband and wife get a partner better than they deserve. Think about it!

It's not called arranged marriages, but there have been parents who have done just that. Through parental intimidation, and because of

Personal Gain

personal covetousness, many a parent has ruined the future of their son or daughter due to personal ambition for wealth.

In the Bible during the reign of the Kings, there is a period when, with close study you will find that marriages during the time frame of Ahab, Athaliah and Omri, were more strategic alliances in an effort to unite the ten northern tribes of Israel with the two southern tribes, and the Lord sent Jehu to wipe them all out.

I had been married to Terri for about a year, having graduated from Bible School, when we left to go out and serve the Lord Jesus Christ. Before heading west, from Pensacola, Florida, we decided that we would take a short trip to southern Florida, and visit Terri's father. It was the first time I had spent any time with him, and all in all things went well.

He owned and managed a nursing home, which took up a lot of his time. In the evenings we would talk, and he would question me about what I was getting ready to do. Of course to him it did not seem all that sensible. I was leaving to go west to work with a man in starting a church in California.

He asked me if I had any savings, and I told him that I did not. He asked if I had any kind of trade experience, and I told him that I did not, though I did tell him that I am not afraid of work, and I had always been able to find work.

He asked me if I would stay there and work for

him. That I could save up the money, and then leave with something in the bank. As he suggested that to me, I immediately thought that it was not right because I was convinced that the Lord wanted me to go to California. Consequently I believed that it was not of the Lord, and there would be no way I was going to stay there and work for him. I thanked him for the offer, but then told him that I was sure the Lord wanted us to go out west.

Thankfully, he was a reasonable man and did not get upset, nor critical with me. To this day though, I am so glad that I did not go to work for my father-in-law. It just seemed like a no win situation to me.

You had better be careful if you are in a family business. If you are a parent or a grandparent in a family business, you had better be careful that you don't cause a son or daughters' marriage to end in divorce. Their marriage is not to be sacrificed on the altar of the family business. Do I see a Laban here? Mom, or Dad, are you a Laban?

In such a situation, an in-law will sacrifice the spirituality of their son or daughters' marriage just for a dollar bill. It doesn't matter that the son or daughter wants to go to church and make sure that their children are in church. What matters to mom or dad is that there is work to do at the shop, and they must be at the shop working. To them, church doesn't pay the bills, and church is not important, what is important is the bottom line, a dollar. The problem is that their god is a dollar bill.

I was holding revival meetings in a church from Sunday through Wednesday. It was a very small congregation in a church in a city down south. Each evening it would get close to the time to start the services, and the song leader was not there. Then it would get a few minutes past the starting time, and the pastor would say, *"So and so will be here shortly. He had to work a little late."* Finally he would show up, a bit harried, and the services would begin. He and his wife had a great desire to be there, and the pastor knew it, but daddy, at the family business, did not care if there was revival services or not.

At the time the song leader's wife was pregnant, who also worked in the business. She would come in slowly, expressionless, sit down in the pew, and just stare straight ahead with what I call the million mile stare. She was completely exhausted.

Come to find out, the father of the business was working them both, and did not care about church, Bible, or anything spiritual. I was told the father even made sure his son had not graduated from high school so as to keep him reliant on the family business. Daddy would brow beat him and tell him, *"You would never be able to get a job as good as this one if you leave."*

As good as that one? Why the guy was working eighty hours a week! Do I see a Laban?

A bad in-law will use you to make money. And if they are lost, that is all the more reason to get out of there. Don't be yoked up with unbelievers.

Jacob stays for the money.

> Gen. 30:25 And it came to pass, when Rachel had born Joseph, that Jacob said unto Laban, Send me away, that I may go unto mine own place, and to my country. Gen. 30:31 And he said, What shall I give thee? And Jacob said, Thou shalt not give me any thing: if thou wilt do this thing for me, I will again feed and keep thy flock.

Jacob stays for the money, and even though it appears to be a mistake, the Lord blessed him. The Lord may not do that for you. If the Lord is telling you to get out, then you had better get out. Don't you use your in-laws to make money off of either. If the Lord lets you and shows you that it is His perfect will, then that is alright. I'm not saying it can't be done. I'm saying that if the Lord tells you to get away then you had better get away. If the relationship is not going well then the Lord may be telling you to get out of there.

Over the years it has been common for me to see a pastor bring his married son, or married daughter into the ministry of his church. Is it the Lord? Maybe! It's not for me to judge. But

Personal Gain

for any young man, whether the pastor is his father or father-in-law, that is a difficult situation. If it is the Lord's will then all is fine. If it is a pastor who is working things out in his own strength it can be very hard. I'm not saying he is a bad man, backslidden or such like. I have just seen pastors work things out in their own strength to bring family into a ministry.

Dear reader, if this is you, there is one thing you must do. You must do what YOU BELIEVE God wants you to do regardless of what anyone else says you should do. Obviously God will not lead you to go against the word of God, but you must obey your Lord Jesus Christ first.

What I am about to write is very delicate but it must be said. If you are serving in a church where a father or father-in-law is the pastor, there is a good chance that you will be accused of being backslidden and rebellious. You will be accused of going against the word of God by not obeying your pastor. If you believe the Lord Jesus Christ is leading you to leave, then you must obey your Saviour.

You just have to go one way or the other.

> No man can serve two masters: for either he will hate the one, and love the other; or else he will hold to the one, and despise the other. Ye cannot serve God and mammon.
> (Matt. 6:24)

Whether it is a family business, or a "family" ministry, be careful.

Dealing With Bad In-Laws

2

No Respect

And said, For this cause shall a man leave father and mother, and shall cleave to his wife: and they twain shall be one flesh? (Matt. 19:5)

Marriage, and the family unit have been instituted by God. It is the basic unit of society. When marriage fails, so too, a society fails and thus degrades into lawlessness. For a daily illustration just look around and see the debauchery that prevails.

I must be careful not to get side tracked here, but the purpose of marriage is to avoid fornication.

Nevertheless, *to avoid* fornication, let every man have his own wife, and let every woman have her own husband. (1Cor. 7:2)

Dealing With Bad In-Laws

As marriage declines, fornication and adultery, along with diseases and such like are on the major increase. The sexual desires of a man and a woman are to be satisfied within marriage.

The marriage and family unit are to be an independent unit before God. That means no one has the authority over your family except the husband and wife. In-laws do not have any authority by God to step into your home and give orders. Let me repeat that. In-laws do not have any authority by God to step into your home and give orders.

A bad in-law will not acknowledge, nor respect your family unit. They will barge right in and start running things, or giving orders whether they have been invited or not. When that takes place they are showing that they have NO REPSECT for either their son or daughter, and their spouse. Before God, they are out of bounds.

> And Laban answered and said unto Jacob, *These* daughters *are* my daughters, and *these* children *are* my children, and *these* cattle *are* my cattle, and all that thou seest *is* mine: and what can I do this day unto these my daughters, or unto their children which they have born? (Gen. 31:43)

Do you see Laban's attitude towards Jacob? Do you see Laban's lack of acknowledgement of Jacob's family unit?

"*These* daughters *are* my daughters." No they're not

Laban, those are Jacobs' wives. (God allowed multiple wives in the Old Testament but not in the New Testament. That is why it says, A Bishop must be the husband of one wife. (1 Tim. 3:2) *"These* children *are* my children." No they're not Laban, those are Jacobs' children. "And all that thou seest *is* mine." No, it's not Laban. All that thou seest is Jacob's!

Laban does not see nor acknowledge Jacobs family unit, and as such Laban is a bad in-law. Hey, son or daughter, your family is an independent unit before God. You are not to have any outside authority running your home. The husband and his wife, with the husband as the head of his home, are the only authority designated by God. The only other authorities I should mention are the laws of the land enforced by the Sheriffs department and the Lord Jesus Christ. But for the context of this book, suffice it to say, you are not to have any outside authority running your home.

Moms and Dads, Moms-in law and Dads-in-law have NO AUTHORITY in your home. You may ask, *"According to who?"* According to God, who is the one that instituted marriage.

> Therefore shall a man leave his father and his mother, and shall cleave unto his wife: and they shall be one flesh. (Gen. 2:24)

The problem comes when Mom or Dad or both, don't even acknowledge that there is a separation. They look at your home as their home, and that is a big problem.

I was preaching a meeting, and afterwards the pastor had us over to his house for food and fellowship. He and his wife are real nice people who love the Lord Jesus Christ and are faithful in their service for him.

We pulled up in front of an upper middle class home in a city. As such the houses had fenced in back yards with one fence separating each property. Each house had a drive way, which was located right beside the driveway of the other house. As we got out of the car we could hear rock and roll music coming from behind the house next door. In the back yard of the next door neighbors house was a swimming pool with teen age boys and girls around it. The noise of the music was mixed with screams and such as they played in the pool. Thankfully, upon entering the pastors' house the noise from the neighbors was shut out when the door was closed.

We enjoyed a good meal with them and had good conversation. I noticed though, that when he would talk about events of the past he would mention that he did it with, "Me and my son, we went and did this. Me and my son, we went and did this also." The conversation consisted quite a bit of memories about him and his son. While there is nothing wrong with doing things with your son, his emphasis seemed a bit out of the norm, you might say. Even when he spoke of future plans they would include "he and his son." Even though his son was grown and married this pastor spoke as if he and his son were one unit.

Then during the conversation he mentioned the noise next door, and how they were bugging him. He couldn't even enjoy his back yard, unless the neighboring people were gone. I agreed that it would be something that could get under your skin, so to speak. Then he seemed to grit his teeth a little, and it was obvious he was a bit upset, or you might say frustrated. Then he asked me, *"You know what, preacher?"* I responded, *"No! What?"*

He said that he used to own that house next door. With great emotion, though not out of control, he said that he gave that house to his son when he got married. His face then grimaced and he said, *"But she, (his daughter-in-law), was not right with God. She got complaining, and one day I came home and the house was put up for sale, with out them even telling me."*

What was going on was that her father-in-law, who was the pastor, would call or go over to their house every day. Without knocking he would walk right into their house. Naturally, she wanted her husband; not her husband and her father-in-law. It was as if they may as well have lived in the same house. He would also discipline their kids just as if they were his. It was a wonder to me that the marriage of his son and daughter-in-law was still together. The young lady had been through many trials because of that father-in-law, and they weren't over when we were there.

It's no wonder she wanted out of there. No doubt that house, though given to them, was a prison, and nothing that even resembled a home to her. They moved away but were still in the same area, and still attended the church. What was needed was for that son to put his foot down and stop the intrusion into their family unit. (There was a family business involved as well.) That father, even though he was a pastor, did not see, nor acknowledge their family unit. He was out of Biblical line, and the son needed to make his father acknowledge his limits in their home. If he would not, then they needed to move far, far away.

If you are married, then you need to realize that you ARE TO LEAVE your father and mother. You are no longer UNDER their authority. I have heard preachers preach that children are to obey their parents, even after they are married. All I have to say is, you have got to be crazy! Honor them, yes! Obey them, no! That Bible says that no man can serve two masters. It all boils down to authority, and God gave the man to be the head over the woman, and the head of his home. If he is the head of his home, then the next step over him is the government and God, but not his father, mother, or in-laws.

I am a Baptist, and as such I believe that the local church is an independent unit that should have no outside authority over it. There is no head office with officers and managers over a local church. The next step over the church is God almighty, but on this earth it is to be an independent unit. Just as your home is to be an independent unit before God on this earth.

As an independent unit then the man is to be the head of his home. Husbands you are no longer a child, a little boy, you are a man. You are an adult, a big person, do you understand? If Mom or Dad tell you what to do, you have the authority to tell them that you will not do it, if you do not think that it is right, or what you think should be done.

At the website: "www.ihatemyinlaws.com" there is some foul language on the site, which I did not appreciate, so I limited my reading of the stories there. I did notice that in most of the cases, the problems would be solved if the son, who was now married, would stand up and be a man, and protect his wife from the junk that she was having to unjustly endure.

Here is one of the stories from the web site:

> MIL (mother-in-law: my added note) i am so sick and tired of you "Telling me" how i should attend every funtion you have, including the

ones where we are not invited by your friends but we should tag along with you since we are all your "kids". I am not your child, DH (meaning her dearest husband - my added note) is and I am not happy going to these stupid functions because i like to NOT!! Rather you and FIL (father-in-law: my added note) have brainwashed DH to think that he needs to go to these stupid dinner parties. Sure it is fun for you but these old _____ friends of yours only use you all. Don't you get it? Any retard can see it?!

I also love how you call Dh and explain to him he has to be at home for dinner tonite and instead of just letting him tell me you have to call me PERSONALLY to tell me...."i don't know if you are going to your families house for dinner but....DH is coming home for dinner. Oh dear we would love for you to come to..but if not we understand." You know what i want to say to that.... _____ _____ darling MIL.

I am tired of you bullying your way into my life. DH is not 5 years old where he has to go where you want him to, wear the clothes only you approve of and god forbid he go to my families house! I can't handle your overbearing personality.

i can say NO to you and then i too will have Happy Days...

(Ihatemyinlaws.com: Posted on Mon, Oct. 23, 2006)

Now there is a prime example of in-laws who do not acknowledge their sons marriage as an independent unit. They are causing great trouble in that marriage, and the son needs to stand up and be a man and block his parents unwanted intrusion into their marriage. If he does not do that chances are he will not have a marriage in a few years.

His wife is suffering needlessly because of his lack of realization that he is to leave his father and mother and cleave unto his wife. If his home ends in divorce it will not be his parents fault directly, it will be his fault for not being the man that he should be. Grow up son, you are no longer a little boy!

Notice what Jacob says to Laban: "Give *me* my wives and my children, for whom I have served thee, and let me go: for thou knowest my service which I have done thee."(Gen. 30:26) Jacob has to ask him for his wives. Can you imagine that? Think about what a situation that must have been, to have to ask for your wives. Those are your wives and children, not Laban's! A bad in-law will try to possess and control everything. All you are is a procreator, but after that it is all his, or hers if it is a mother-in-law.

There is a story of a young man who got married, and about two weeks after they were married he and his bride got in a heated disagreement. That is also known as a fight. Well now, that is natural. There is a time where you both have to learn to live with each other. Sure, you love each other, but now you must learn to live with each other and like each other.

His young bride was working a job, and after work she decided that she would go home to where she used to live two weeks earlier, which was her parents house.

She arrived at the house and went inside. Evening was setting in, and it appeared that she was going to stay the night. Her father, sitting in his chair in the living room, (I don't know if he was a saved man or not, but he had good sense), looked across the room at her and asked, "*What are you doing here?*" She told him that she and _____ had a fight, and that she was going to spend the night there. Her father then sternly said to her, "*Oh no, you're not! You go get in your car and go home to your husband.*"

That young lady had a good man for a father. That was the right thing to say. He acknowledged the family unit and enforced it on his daughter. He greatly helped his son-in-law that night.

No Respect

Let me give you one more story about this. Remember, a bad in-law will not respect nor acknowledge your family unit. As such they will intrude right into your life with out a second thought. To them your marriage is their business, and you are still their little boy or girl who ought to obey them blindly. To that you can say, "Nuts!"

I heard the story of a Christian family. And this is a good christian family in full time service for the Lord Jesus Christ. There is no doubt that they love the Lord, and have made many sacrifices in their service for Him.

Their daughter married a fine young man whom the Lord Jesus Christ called to be a missionary. After graduating from Christian school, they did deputation (raised support) and left for the mission field that God had called him to. The field was very far away, half way around the world. While there they had a heavy trial placed upon them. After much consideration and no doubt prayer, they came to a decision.

The problem was that the decision they came to was contrary to her mother and fathers beliefs. It was not a doctrinal decision, but a practical one. When her mother found out about what they were planning to do, she bought a plane ticket and flew half way around the world, went up to where they were, and told them they would not do such, and that they would do it her way. To this they changed their decision and submitted to mother-in-laws' demand.

Now that young man, I'm sure is a good man, but he needed to step in and tell his mother-in-law, *"Mom, we love you and we know you mean well. But we will not do it your way for this is none of your business. Get out of here and leave us alone!"*

The very idea of her going and telling him what they will or won't do. The very idea. She had no authority to do that, and he had all the Biblical authority to tell her, *"No, we will not!"* Hey Mom, how about you praying and letting God tell them what to do?

That may sound harsh, and I'm sure it is, but I want you to know that these cases I am referring to are when the other more civil approaches have been tried. Ideally, you want to have a good relationship with your in-laws, as well as your own parents. That is the best way. But that is not always possible, and you need to realize that there are God given boundaries around your marriage that no one has a right to infringe upon.

3

Can't Please Them

Gen 31:38 This twenty years *have* I *been* with thee; thy ewes and thy she goats have not cast their young, and the rams of thy flock have I not eaten. 39 That which was torn *of beasts* I brought not unto thee; <u>I bare the loss of it</u>;(Emphasis Added) of my hand didst thou require it, *whether* stolen by day, or stolen by night. 40 *Thus* I was; in the day the drought consumed me, and the frost by night; and my sleep departed from mine eyes. 41 *Thus* have I been twenty years in thy house; I served thee fourteen years for thy two daughters, and six years for thy cattle: and thou hast changed my wages ten times. 42 Except the God of my father, the God of Abraham, and the fear of Isaac, had been with me, surely thou hadst sent me away now empty.

Notice in the passage the grief that Laban put Jacob through. In verse 39 notice, "I bare the loss of it." Whatever went wrong Laban required it to come out of Jacob's paycheck. It is obvious from the passage that Jacob tried as much as he was able to please Laban, but it was not possible. Based upon Gen. 31:29 It is in the power of my hand to do you hurt, that Laban had been trying to destroy Jacob so all that Jacob had would be his. Another example of personal gain involved. It also appears that Jacob let Laban walk all over him, so to speak, for twenty years.

YOU CAN NEVER PLEASE A BAD IN LAW NO MATTER HOW HARD YOU TRY!

John's mother-in-law was a devout Greek Orthodox. John and his wife were devout Bible Believing Baptists. The combination was like oil and vinegar. But they had a burden to see her get saved and truly born again. They wondered if she might be saved, but after lengthy discussions it was obvious that her faith was in her "good works" through her church and not in Jesus Christ alone.

With this on their hearts they wanted to do all they could in order to win her to a saving knowledge of our Lord Jesus Christ. They tried all that they could do, within reason, to please her, but the more they tried to please her the less respect she had for them, especially for John. This was on top of the friction that was already present from John taking her baby girl away. At times John found himself wondering what to do about it all. He was just trying to be a good testimony and at the same time trying to be on good terms with his mother-in-law. It didn't work!

The thought of her going to Hell pressed upon both of them to be patient and to put up with the trouble that she was causing, but no matter what they did she was either angry or upset about something all of the time. John realized that she was never going to respect him and because of it she was never going to listen to what he had to say. It had come to the point where a decision had to be made. John thought to himself, "We have talked to her about salvation at least three times, but it is now time to move on. She will never be pleased no matter what we do."

I know a pastor's wife who got a phone call one day from a lady in their church. This lady was a faithful wife, Christian and enjoyed serving the Lord Jesus Christ. But out of frustration she gave the pastors' wife a call mainly just to have someone to talk to. When the pastors' wife asked her how she was doing she said, *"Not well. My mother is driving me crazy, and now it is starting to affect my marriage."*

What was going on was that they had brought her mother to live with them into their small three bedroom one bath home. They had two boys at the time, both of which were teenagers. The boys would often hit, kick or provoke each other. With mother coming into the home, the boys were now both in the same bedroom. Along with this strife, was the fact that her mother was a complainer. She would gripe and gripe to her daughter all day long. No matter what she did, mom would gripe to her. The day she called she said that she did not know what she was going to do. It was getting so bad that it was starting to effect their marriage.

The pastors wife said that she knew what was needed to be done. Surprised, but open to advice she asked what should I do? *"You need to get her out of your home. Find a place for her to stay on her own,"* was the reply. The mother was healthy, could take care of herself, but could not drive.

I am not saying that you should neglect your parents, that is not what I am saying. But here was a case where there was needless effort being put out to accommodate her mom, and it was needless at the time.

When her husband got home from work that evening she told him what had been suggested, and they did just that. They found an assisted living apartment, and moved her into it, and that greatly helped their marriage, their boys, the home and all. They still went by and checked on her every day, took her to church with them and had her over for dinner often. As I said before, I am not suggesting neglecting them, but there must be some understanding of your own needs and responsibilities before God.

They meant well by taking her into their home, but those good intentions could have turned out with bad results had they not moved her out of the home.

Even with all that they had done for her mother, yet she was neither content nor satisfied. You will never please a bad in-law no matter how hard you try, and the very attempt to please them can become a trap for you that once you are in you may not know how to get out of it. So you may wonder what you should do? What you should do is seek to please God first. He is the one that you must FIRST SEEK TO PLEASE. If that does not please your in-laws then that is just too bad for them. You will not give account to them at the judgment, but to God.

> Gen. 31:39 That which was torn *of beasts* I brought not unto thee; I bare the loss of it; of my hand didst thou require it, *whether* stolen by day, or stolen by night. 41 *Thus* have I been twenty years in thy house; I served thee fourteen years for thy two daughters, and six years for thy cattle: and thou hast changed my wages ten times. 42 Except the God of my father, the God of Abraham, and the fear of Isaac, had been with me, surely thou

hadst sent me away now empty.

If there was anyone who tried to please an in-law it was Jacob! You can see from the passage that he did all he could to make Laban happy, and Laban was not happy.

> And your father hath deceived me, and changed my wages ten times; but God suffered him not to hurt me. (Gen. 31:7)

That gives you another glimpse of how bad it was for Jacob. If it were not for God, Laban would have done Jacob hurt. It can get that bad, and you do not have the Covenant of physical blessing that Jacob had which was, "... cursed *be* every one that curseth thee, and blessed *be* he that blesseth thee." (Gen. 27:29b)

I was preaching this sermon one evening at a church of about seventy five people. Most of the regular church members were there that evening as well as some visitors. As a visiting Evangelist often times I do not know who are the visitors and who are the regulars. Nor do I know what all is going on in the lives of the people. I just pray and ask the Lord what He would have me to preach and by His grace I attempt to preach it.

Well, I was preaching this sermon, and I was preaching very strongly. I came to this point of not being able to please a bad in-law no matter how hard you try, when about two thirds of the way back in the church a petite white haired aged sister started to shout. I just kept preaching, and she just kept shouting.

She pulled out a white handkerchief and started waving it in the air, and as she did she was shouting in a petite high grandma voice, "Well, you preach it brother, Amen! Preach it brother, preach it!"

I kind of gathered from her reaction that she had been in the situation where she had tried to please her in-laws, and no matter what she did she could not please them. I'll bet you in years past that she has shed some tears over her in-laws.

4

Destroy Your Marriage

Gen. 31:20 And Jacob stole away unawares to Laban the Syrian, in that he told him not that he fled. 21 So he fled with all that he had; and he rose up, and passed over the river, and set his face *toward* the mount Gilead. 22 And it was told Laban on the third day that Jacob was fled.

Gen. 31:3 And the LORD said unto Jacob, Return unto the land of thy fathers, and to thy kindred; and I will be with thee.

A BAD IN LAW WILL EITHER DESTROY YOUR MARRIAGE, OR ALIENATE THEIR SON OR DAUGHTER.

Dealing With Bad In-Laws

This is a very important truth to understand. You must realize that you can only take so much before something has to give. With enough external pressure something is going to break! And I must say that what is needed is for the man of the home to step up and deal with the external pressure. The resolving of the trouble rests on the man. The solution to the trouble begins with the man. He must realize his duty to his wife and children, and he must realize what the biblical and proper boundaries are for his marriage and family. Until that takes place there very likely will be no solution to the problem.

As the trouble persists, if it is not dealt with, it will become more of a burden the longer it goes on. The person that will receive the brunt of it all will be the wife. It is the wife that will shed the most tears, and have the broken heart. It doesn't matter if it is her parents or his, generally she will be effected the most.

The reason for this is that the woman is the weaker vessel so it will get to her more, and Satan often works on the woman to get to the man. That is what he did in the garden, and that is what he did with Job, David, Solomon, etc. and that is what he will do in your marriage. He will use whatever he can to split up your home, and in-laws are one of the ways he works to destroy the home.

Another reason trouble with in-laws effects

the woman more is that her desire is to her husband. God made her that way. The relationship a wife has with her husband is very important to her. God said that her desire would be to her husband.

> Unto the woman he said, I will greatly multiply thy sorrow and thy conception; in sorrow thou shalt bring forth children; and thy desire *shall be* to thy husband, and he shall rule over thee. (Gen. 3:16)

So when something like in-laws start to get between a wife and husband it is the wife who suffers the most. When the husband does not deal with the situation then his wife can feel abandoned, betrayed, and all alone with no one to turn to. Her desire is for her husband to stand up for her, to defend her. She wants to see him seek to prevent anything from coming between them, including in-laws. When he does not do this, nor even attempt to do this she is hurt deep down inside. In her view, she is now second choice in his heart.

In the situation with in-laws you have one of two choices to make. You can side with your parents, or you can side with your spouse. You MUST go one way or the other, and IT IS GOD'S WILL FOR YOU TO SIDE WITH YOUR SPOUSE! As the stress grows, so too the point of breaking becomes ever greater.

Mom and Dad, don't you dare help break up a marriage. Back off and give them space. You will be able to see your grand children and things will go much better. But if you keep the pressure on then something will have to break.

I was talking to a pastor whose daughter had been recently married. She and her husband were members of this pastor's church, and it was a very good working relationship. The pastor told me that he missed his daughter as they were very close. He wanted to go out to lunch with her, but instead of asking her, he went to his son-in-law and asked him if he could go out to lunch with his daughter. I thought to myself, that is a good pastor and father-in-law. What's more is that he gets to spend time with his daughter because he respects his son-in-law's authority over his own home.

The Bible says,

> No man can serve two masters: for either he will hate the one, and love the other; or else he will hold to the one, and despise the other. (Matt. 6:24)

There has been many a young lady who loves her mom and dad, but also loves her husband. As her parents tell her one thing she tries to please them, only to find that her husband disagrees and wants it another way, so she tries to please him. Her parents get upset that she disobeyed them and brow beat her down. Then she finds that her husband is upset with them and how they are treating her. She tries to smooth it over, and the cycle goes on and on until one day she either breaks, or chooses.

You need to choose, and you are to choose your husband, and if need be go against your parents. If you are not able to stand up to your parents then your husband is to stand up to them for you. YOU CAN NOT, YOU CAN NOT, YOU CAN NOT serve two masters, is that clear? That is what God said on the matter.

If you are afraid of what daddy will do, or mommy, because you know, they are going to get mad. Then you must realize that you are a big person now. You are not a little child anymore. It is time for you to run your own life with the help of God, and without the unsolicited interference of in-laws.

I have known people who, even though they lived in a fairly close proximity to their in-laws, had to stay away from them. The one family I know was very polite and honored his mother and father when in their presence, but because of the contention between them they never would purposely go around them.

One such example was John and Lisa who had met, and were married their second year of Bible School. While in their third year of school, Lisa gave birth to a baby boy. They were very happy and thrilled to be serving the Lord Jesus Christ. Unfortunately Lisa's mother was not of the same faith. She would call Lisa daily and critique John and his decisions. Because Lisa's mother was lost they would put up with her ridicule, complaints and such with the hope of witnessing to her one day so that she would be saved and go to Heaven when she died.

The months turned into years and yet Lisa's mother would call, complain and tell Lisa all that she was doing wrong. More than once Lisa would be in tears by the end of a phone call, kneel down on her knees and pray to God for grace. John would try to comfort her and tell her that she was doing a great job but it frustrated John seeing his wife go through the sorrow that she was.

John knew that he ought to put his foot down, but in his mind he thought, "Who was he to tell Lisa's mother what to do or not, after all that was her mother."

The Bible says,

> Likewise, ye husbands, dwell with them according to knowledge, giving honour unto the wife, as unto the weaker vessel, and as being heirs together of the grace of life; that your prayers be not hindered.
> (1Pet. 3:7)

What John came to realize, though it was twenty years into their marriage, was that his dear wife Lisa was not able to stand up to her mother. No matter how hard she tried to put her foot down it didn't work. Her mother would just ignore her and proceed with what she was going to do anyway. Lisa needed her husband to step in and one day he finally did just that.

With authority in his voice and determination in his spirit he told Lisa and the children, "We are done with your mother. All communication is over." That was very hard for John to do but he did it.

You know what surprised him? About one month after making that decision Lisa came up to him and thanked him. She said, "For the first time in my life I feel alive, and I am finally free.

A bad in-law will either destroy the marriage, or they will alienate their son or daughter. It is God's will for you to go with your spouse.

I know a man who was married and has two children. He and his, then wife, had a great marriage and family with two children under the age of ten years old. They loved each other and there was a joy and happiness in their home.

One day after church they asked us over to their house to enjoy a meal with them and we accepted their offer and went. It was a good time of spiritual fellowship. I noticed though that upon entering their house there were toys for the children all over the place. It was not a messy disorganized house. It was due to the amount of toys that they had. It was almost to the point of trails through the living room with toys being lined on each side. There was no room to put the toys away, and it was not an overly small house. I think it was a three bedroom two bath house. An average middle class American home.

77

During the course of the visit, perhaps he noticed our glances at the amount of toys, I don't know, but he said that he had told his in-laws to not buy any more toys, but they would not listen. Her parents lived in the same town and there was a constant contact with them.

In the course of time he believed that God was leading him to go to Bible School. He packed up and moved with his family a couple thousand miles away to go to Bible School. He was excited and glad to be there, but she was not all that excited and happy to be there.

Once a year, during the summer, her parents paid for her and the children to come back and visit them for a few weeks. It might have been a month at a time. The first year they did this, as well as calling her very often and talking to her.

He would try to limit the calls and visits, but his wife was not cooperating by this time. Toys continued to arrive, trips were made back home and his third and last year of school, the in-laws paid for her and the kids to come home, and they never came back.

His marriage was destroyed, and in part because his in-laws enabled her to leave him. There was a choice to be made, and God's will was for her to obey, and to stay with her husband. He loved her, was true to her, yet she kept listening to her mother and father and ended up making the wrong choice.

You can not serve two masters and sooner or later you will arrive at a breaking point where a decision has to be made. You will either be alienated from your parents or you will leave your spouse. It is God's will for you to be alienated from your parents, for it certainly is not God's will for you to leave your spouse.

Dealing With Bad In-Laws

5

Solution is Distance

Gen. 31:20 And Jacob stole away unawares to Laban the Syrian, in that he told him not that he fled. 21 So he fled with all that he had; and he rose up, and passed over the river, and set his face *toward* the mount Gilead.

Men - *your wife comes before your mom or dad.*

(Posted on ihatemyinlaws.com 9.09.2015)

A few weeks ago, I posted a story about how I had a massive go at all my in-laws in a dream. Well, I just had a nap and dreamt I had another go at them but this time it was toned down and I might of just got away with it in real life.

Food for thought should I ever [reach my] breaking point with these useless idiots and give them a piece of my mind one day. These people put me in such h___ and my husband only semi stands up for me (he picks and chooses when to do so.)

Perhaps that breaking point day may come quicker than expected...

Granted, this is only one side of the story, yet it illustrates how a woman, a wife, longs for and needs her husband to take care of the situation. To her, she is coming in second place and it hurts. And might I say she is right about the matter.

Ladies - *Your husband comes before your mom or dad.*

There must be boundaries set up between your family and your In laws, but it is going to take the man to set them up and enforce them. Maybe there is an exception to this statement where a wife can do this, but that will be the exception. The vast majority of the time it will take the husband to establish the boundaries so that his immediate family has privacy, rest and peace.

In this age men are discouraged from being men. The press, educational system and many of the laws of the land are such that a man has an uphill battle in order just to be a man, a husband and a father. I am not whining, that is just how it is, but because of this there are many men who just do not know what to do in these situations. "When the wicked rise, a man is hidden. (Prov. 28:12)

What's more is that there are many men today who were never around their father when they were growing up and have no idea how to be a father and husband. This is where it is a great help and advantage if you are a Christian and have the word of God to read, for it tells you what the responsibilities of the man are, as well as what the responsibilities of the woman are, as well as the children. If you have the Bible then you have the proper instructions on how to set up your home.

Your home is an independent unit and has to have boundaries set. If there are no boundaries in your home, and in your marriage, then you are extremely vulnerable to attack, and there is a Devil who seeks to destroy marriages and families. The marriage is a spiritual institution that Satan desires to destroy. You need boundaries established to protect your marriage and family. A secure and happy home is not just an accident. It doesn't just happen automatically. It is the result of proper effort and work to establish and preserve your home.

If in-laws, friends or others do not understand

where the boundaries are, then as the man and the head of your home you need to make them understand where those boundaries are. In regards to in-laws, you are going to have to deal with them one way or another. If you have tried to talk to them, or if you have written them and they are not listening to your demands, then your actions must become more serious in nature.

No, I am not; I am not saying to get a gun, pepper spray, taser, or another weapon of self defense. At times you may have wanted to do this, but that is not an option, unless it is truly a matter of self defense. Jacob had God defend him, for God told Laban that if you say anything good or bad to Jacob then I will kill you.

> 24 Take heed that thou speak not to Jacob either good or bad. Gen. 31:29 It is in the power of my hand to do you hurt: but the God of your father spake unto me yesternight, saying, Take thou heed that thou speak not to Jacob either good or bad. (Gen. 31:24, 29)

It is implied that God would kill him.

It can get to the point of violence, and I am sure the police have answered many calls in regards to relatives fighting. You must be sober and guard your family.

I had a man tell me that he got information that his mother-in-law had reported him to children's services and that in all likelihood the next day they were coming to his house. That meant there was a very good chance that they would remove the children from their home.

This was a Christian home with love and joy, it was not a weird religious sect with strange activities. It was, and is a loving family. But Grandma did not like a strong man in charge and thought it wrong. That night the husband said, *"Pack it up we are leaving,"* and they left in the middle of the night. Grandma, who reported them, would not listen, she would not respect the boundaries, so they left and that was the right thing to do. She lost all contact with them for quite a long time. They moved almost two thousand miles away.

If in-laws are destroying your home then God will command you to get away from them. The Lord told Jabob to get out and go back to his family. But if you study it out, when he gets back there his father dies, and he has nothing to do with his brother Esau. Even though Jacob goes home, he is still on his own.

Notice also that the Bible says that he "fled." He was fleeing a very oppressive and unhappy situation. That might be what you have to do.

Did you notice that Abraham did not get blessed until Lot was out of the picture. God wanted him totally separated from all of his relatives. That probably won't be true for you, and it is likely that if you understand the boundaries of your home, and if your In laws understand them as well, and respect them, then you will likely have a great relationship with them. But this small book is on a bad in-law, and as such if you have a bad in-law then you will have to separate your self from them.

Notice Laban's attitude towards Jacob.

> And Laban answered and said unto Jacob, *These* daughters *are* my daughters, and *these* children are my children, and these cattle *are* my cattle, and all that thou seest is mine: and what can I do this day unto these my daughters, or unto their children which they have born?
>
> (Gen. 31:43)

Laban is frustrated, for God told him the night before not say say anything good or bad to Jacob. So now Laban has no power, but look what he says, "What can I do..." he was prepared to do something and Jacob was right when he said, "Except the God of my father, the God of Abraham, and the fear of Isaac, had been with me, surely thou hadst sent me away now empty." (Gen. 31:42) Laban had come to take back what Laban assumed was his, but God stopped him. So now that Laban sees he can not prevail, then he makes a deal with Jacob. The little bit here in the word of God illustrates Laban's attitude toward Jacob.

Laban says, "J...J...Jacob." Laban had a hard time saying his name. *"Hey, ...uh, Jacob, how about you and I making an agreement."*

Jacob: ever attempting and open for peace

Solution Is Distance

cautiously replies, "What do you have in mind?"

Laban: "Well, how about you and I setting up a heap of stones here and let it be for a witness that we will not cross this line to each other for harm."

Jacob: "That is fine with me. I would be more than happy to participate in such an agreement."

Laban: "Good. So lets erect a heap of stones and we will make the agreement."

To Jacob this was a change from what he had been used to. Laban was actually working with him. What's more is that there would be a barrier between each other which excited Jacob. So Jacob started gathering and assembling the stone monument. He was so excited about the thought of being rid of Laban as well as the mutual agreement that he didn't even notice that he was the one doing all of the work.

"And Jacob took a stone, and set it up *for* a pillar." (Gen. 31:45) Then, looking up he saw that Laban and his men were all sitting around and watching Jacob work. "And Jacob said unto his brethren, Gather stones." (Gen. 31:46) How about some of you getting off your rear ends and helping me with this? With grunts and gripes murmured under their breath, Laban's men pitched in to help. It took Jacob getting on them in order for him to get some help.

Once the heap of witness was finished, Laban, who had not lifted a finger to help, spoke up and took control of the ceremony and proclaimed:

"This heap is a witness between me and thee this day. The Lord watch between me and thee, when we are absent one from another. If thou shalt afflict my daughters, or if thou shalt take *other* wives beside my daughters, no man *is* with us; see, God *is* witness betwixt me and thee." (Gen. 31:48-50)

Now watch what he says, "And Laban said to Jacob, Behold this heap, and behold *this* pillar, which I have cast betwixt me and thee." (Gen. 31:51) Laban hadn't done a thing. Jacob was the one sweating. This heap be witness, and this pillar be witness, that I will not pass over this heap to thee, and that thou shalt not pass over this heap and this pillar unto me, for harm.

Laban then says to Jacob, " *Jacob will you swear before God to this agreement?*" Jacob then says, "*I swear to it by the fear of my father Isaac."* Then as Jacob waits for Laban to swear and do his part, it never comes. Laban never swears. To swear over something in the Old Testament was to put yourself under a curse. A curse as such if you did not perform what you swore. Laban got Jacob to build the heap, swear over it, and then Laban said good-bye. Laban takes control of that whole situation there and then leaves. It gives a clear picture of what Jacob had been dealing with for those twenty years. Laban had absolutely no respect for Jacob, and in a practical sense, God told Jacob

Solution Is Distance

to get away from his father-in-law.

If you are having trouble with in-laws, and you have tried to talk to them and work the problems out, yet it is to no avail, then you must sever the relationship. Ask the Lord to help you. And it must begin with the man, for the wife can not do it. I say it must begin with the man, and while that is true, you two must be together on this thing. You must unite in your action, love and marriage. That is God's will for you.

With this being the case, then you must sever the relationship. If need be then that means 500 to 1000 miles separation. Maybe you tried that and they followed you. Then you might try leaving in the middle of the night, and don't let them know you are gone. That is what Jacob did. If they find you again and follow then you might need a restraining order, but one way or the other you must establish a boundary for your marriage and home. It will help you even though it may cost you financially. A happy marriage and home is far more valuable than a large savings account.

When all you have is each other and God, it brings you closer together, which is how it ought to be.

Dealing With Bad In-Laws

6

A Hurting In-Law

Laban was a bad in-law and the practical lessons that I have mentioned in this book concern how to deal with one. But as I got to the end of writing this book I thought of the mothers and fathers who are not bad in-laws and yet they have been excluded from their son or daughter's marriage altogether. There is also the grandparents whose son or daughter has gone through a divorce and now the grandchildren are living with their son in-law or daughter in-law and they have shut the biological grandparents out. There are many other scenarios as well that could be mentioned.

Maybe you have been rejected from seeing your grandchildren, and as you read this book you were frustrated, angry and saying to yourself, *"But I have not been that way. I have stayed out of their business. I loved them and sacrificed myself for them."* Yet, they have "locked" you out of their life and you are not even able to see your grandchildren. Your heart hurts and at times, more often than not, you weep because of it.

It is very frustrating to think that you wiped their rear end, fed them, nursed them when they were sick, paid for their food, bought their clothes and provided a home for them, and then they look at you and say, *"But that's what you were supposed to do."* They then leave and don't want you in their life and you realize you have been used. At least this is how a man often views this. A mothers' heart will be more selfless and rejoice for the opportunity to have cared for her children. The cost to a mother is not usually considered. That is a mothers' heart, and she probably hurts the most.

Yes, many times the in-law trouble in a home comes down from the parents, but there is also the hurt and pain that comes up from unthankful children, or an insecure spouse that makes sure their in-laws are not included in their family at all.

Is it right that such things happen? No, not at all. If this is you, then let me say congratulations upon getting this far in this book and not putting it down, or throwing it at the wall when you got to the Solution chapter. But what are you to do if you are a mom or dad, grandmother or grandfather, and you have been rejected from participating in your children's family. What do you do when you are not even able to see your grandchildren? How are you to deal with that?

The following advice is brief as it would take another book to go into detail about how to deal with such a situation. This advice is from a minister and a Bible perspective.

First and foremost you need to make sure that you are saved! You need to realize your need for the Lord Jesus Christ as your personal Saviour. Why? On the practical side so that you can take your hurt and your burdens to Him.

The word of God says, "Casting all your care upon Him, for he careth for you." (1 Peter 5:7) You are not to drown your pain in booze, tranqulizers, dope or any other form of escape. There will be no help in alternative medicine either. Energy Psychology, acupuncture, suggestive tapping and other similar techniques are nothing more that witchcraft. There may be a temporary comfort and help from such practices, but the help won't last and will only draw you into a pit of nervousness, fear and depression, just the same as booze or drugs.

The right place to go to for refuge is Jesus

Christ. As the old song goes, *"The Lord's our Rock, in Him we hide, a shelter in the time of storm."*

With Jesus Christ as your Saviour you have a place to go to, and a person who understands rejection. You can go to Him in prayer and tell Him all about your problems and He cares for you. He is not too busy for you, because He loves you. The Lord Jesus Christ knows all about rejection for He was rejected and crucified while being innocent.

The second thing you must do is to forgive them. This does not mean act like nothing is wrong. It means you must choose to forgive them before God. Don't let what they have done to you destroy your relationship with Jesus Christ. That is what the Devil wants to happen. You must forgive them between you and God, and it may take time to do this.

If you find yourself with thoughts of vengeance, or if you find yourself with your mind/heart bringing up memories that hurt and make you cry, and if your mind is constantly thinking about what they have done to you, how to fix it, or if you are just plain consumed with the situation, then you need to get with the Lord Jesus Christ and forgive them. Yes, there will be a constant burden on your heart that you will carry from day to day. You love them, and you will always love them, but you must not be consumed with the situation. Through Jesus Christ and the word of God you can rise above the pain. That doesn't mean the pain won't be there, it just means that you can move on with your life without letting the pain destroy you.

Find a place where you know you are alone and no one will hear you. Get away from your phone, computer, television, and people. Kneel, if you are able, close your eyes and pray out loud. Jesus said, "When thou prayest, enter into thy closet." (Matt. 6:6) Get alone with the Lord Jesus Christ, talk to Him and tell Him everything that is on your heart. This is going to take some time, tears and tissues. After telling Jesus Christ all about it then, as best as you can, surrender and forgive them. Make sure what they have done to you does not destroy you, or your relationship with Jesus Christ.

Lastly, and I do not want to sound hard but you need to get your own life. So many parents end up with their life all wrapped up in their children and when the children are grown and gone they don't know what to do. Well, depending on how many children you raised, the past twenty years has been spent raising children, especially if you are a mother.

So now the children are grown and gone. They have lives of their own, and they don't want you in their lives. Then there is someone who does want you in His life. It is Jesus Christ and He has work for you to do. Get busy doing what you were created to do which is to find out the job the Lord Jesus Christ has for you to do and get busy doing it. There is not a greater privilege than that and there is no doubt that Jesus Christ has work for you to do.

One time there was a man who was estranged from his children and consequently his grandchildren. He told me that he cried and cried for many years about it. He, and as well as his wife, were never even told of the birth of the grandchildren. Their hearts were broken, but as they sought Jesus Christ in the matter, He began to give them victory over the pain. As time went on they began to minister to other people who had gone through, or were going through the same thing. Little by little they began to thank the Lord for the trial as they saw that He could now use them to minister to others going through the same thing.

In the book of Hebrews it says, "Lest any root of bitterness springing up trouble *you*." (Heb. 12:15) You have a choice, which is to allow God to make you better, or you can harden yourself and become bitter. The Lord wants to use you for His glory, if you will let him. If you are reading this and have never been born again, then the next chapter is extremely important for you to read. Either way the Lord can take this "curse" and turn it into a blessing, if you will let Him. Don't sit there and wallow in your self pity. You are only destroying yourself.

The Lord Jesus Christ has a will for your life. He has a purpose and work for you to do for Him. There is victory through this trial as you submit to the Lord Jesus Christ.

I am going to write something that right now you may think is impossible, but if you find out what the King of the Universe wants you to do, and you get started doing it, then there may come a day when you will realize the rejection of your children was one of the best things that ever happened to you! You will have a life of your own and it is a life of joy, happiness and eternal purpose. Often, when you get to that point, God allows the relationship to be restored and healed.

Why then? Because He now knows that your children, or grandchildren are not an idol. In your heart Jesus Christ is first as He ought to be.

7

Salvation

Dear friend, would you let me ask you one of the most important questions that you will ever be asked in this life? The question is this, *"Do you know that you are going to Heaven when you die?"*

Perhaps you say that no one knows where they are going when they die. Well, St. Peter knew that he was going to Heaven for he said that he was born again, "kept by the power of God," and that he had an incorruptible inheritance reserved in Heaven. St. John knew that he was going to Heaven for he said,

> 1 John 3:2 "Now are we the sons of God...and we know that we shall be like Him." 1 John 5:13 "These things have I written unto you that believe on the name of the Son of God; that ye may know that ye have eternal life."

Not only did St. Peter and St. John know where they were going when they died, but St. Paul also knew for he said that he had a "desire to depart, and to be with Christ; which is far better." And of course Jesus Christ said, "I go unto my Father."

All of these men, as well as the Son of God, knew where they were going when they died. If they knew, you can know also. In the Bible again St. John wrote, "These things have I written unto you that believe on the name of the Son of God; that ye may know that ye have eternal life." (1 Jn 5:13) Do you know that you have eternal life? Do you know that you are going to Heaven when you die?

Let me start at the very beginning. The person you are going to have to deal with is called, "the Word," and He is the Creator of all things.

> John 1:1 In the beginning was the Word, and the Word was with God, and the Word was God. 2 The same was in the beginning with God. 3 All things were made by him; and without him was not any thing made that was made. 4 In him was life; and the life was the light of men.

He is also righteous. In Heaven they worship Him.

> And the four beasts had each of them six wings about *him*; and *they were* full of eyes within: and they rest not day and night, saying, Holy, holy, holy, Lord God Almighty, which was, and is, and is to come. (Rev. 4:8)

His name is the Son of God, the Lord Jesus Christ.

> But unto the Son *he saith*, Thy throne, O God, *is* for ever and ever: a sceptre of righteousness *is* the sceptre of thy kingdom. (Heb. 1:8)

The Lord Jesus Christ is Holy. That means He has never sinned one time. There is no spot nor blemish in the Lord Jesus Christ. He is absolutely perfect. Along with that, Heaven is also perfect. It is a place of joy, happiness, light, and righteousness. In Heaven:

> Rev. 21:4 And God shall wipe away all tears from their eyes; and there shall be no more death, neither sorrow, nor crying, neither shall there be any more pain: for the former things are passed away. 5 And he that sat upon the throne said, Behold, I make all things new. And he said unto me, Write: for these words are true and faithful.

This is just a glimpse of Heaven but it gives a glimpse of a place where it can honestly be written as an epitaph, *"...and they lived happily ever after."* Doesn't that sound like a place you would like to spend eternity in?

Heaven is beautiful because the God of Heaven is Holy, the place called Heaven is Holy, and the people of Heaven are holy. My desire in writing this is to tell you how you can know when you die you will make it to this beautiful place called Heaven. Then it can be written of you, he or she lived happily ever after.

This brings us to the subject of holiness. Are you holy? Are you righteous? Are you a good person? To answer the first two questions I would think it would be easy to answer, "No." You are not holy, and you are not righteous. But maybe your answer to the third question is a, "Yes." You might say that you are a good person. You're nice to others and try to help folks when you can. That is a good thing.

When it comes to holiness though, how do we judge what is holy? How do we know what holiness is? To answer these two questions we must go back in time about 3500 years to a mountain in Arabia. It is a mountain called Mt. Sinai. On that mountain is a man called Moses. The Lord God has called him there, and camped below in the plain is a nation God has called out of Egypt named Israel.

The top of that mountain, can be seen today in 2016. It is in Arabia and has been burnt black, and is a reminder of the event that I am about to tell you of. Moses went up into the mount and God came down in fire on the top of that mount and gave Moses Ten Commandments. These Ten Commandments are a glimpse of holiness and what holiness is, or should I say, the standard by which holiness is judged. I am going to use only four of the ten and let's see how you measure up to holiness.

Salvation

1. Ex. 20:7 Thou shalt not take the name of the LORD thy God in vain; for the LORD will not hold him guiltless that taketh his name in vain.

This is the third commandment. To take the Lord's name in vain is called blasphemy and it is very serious. Have you ever taken the Lord's name in vain? In other words have you ever said, "Oh my God," or "Jesus Christ," or "Lord God Almighty," or just "Jesus?" If you have ever said any of these in vain, or other variations, how many times in your life have you taken His name in vain? In vain would mean that you just said His name without using it in a sentence, thus in vain. Since this is called blasphemy, then you would be called a blasphemer.

If you have broken this commandment then you are a blasphemer.

2. Ex. 20:15 Thou shalt not steal.

This is the eighth commandment. Have you ever stolen anything in your life? Stop and think about this. Have you ever, without permission, downloaded any music, or anything that was copyrighted? Have you ever taken something that was not yours. Size does not matter. From a piece of candy to millions of dollars, have you ever stolen something?

It doesn't matter what religion you are for these laws are written on your heart. You know instinctively that it is wrong to take something that is not yours.

What does God call someone who steals? They are called a thief. So then if you have stolen anything you are a thief. You are guilty of breaking God's law when He wrote, "Thou shalt not steal."

If you have broken both of these commandments then you are a blasphemer and a thief. Keep in mind this is only two of the ten commandments.

3. Ex. 20:14 Thou shalt not commit adultery.

This is to have sex with someone who is not your spouse, thus it is to have sex outside of marriage. Jesus, who was God manifest in the flesh, went even farther and stated, Matt. 5:28 But I say unto you, That whosoever looketh on a woman to lust after her hath committed adultery with her already in his heart. Adultery is now committed in your heart by looking on someone and lusting after them sexually, as well as the physical act of fornicating with someone. Fornication is what it is called when sex is committed outside of marriage. This would include Sodomy. Have you ever done that?

If you have, even if just once, then you are an adulterer, or could also be called a fornicator. If you have broken all three of these commandments then you are a blasphemer, thief and a fornicator.

The last commandment that I will mention here is this:

Salvation

4. Matt. 19:18 "...Thou shalt not bear false witness."

Also known as, "Thou shalt not lie." Have you ever told a lie? To speak a false witness is to tell a lie. A witness tells what he or she knows. To be a false witness is to not speak or tell the truth about what you know. Have you ever done that? How many times have you done that in your life? 1 time? 10? 100? 1000? Etc.?

A person who tells lies, is called a liar. Then you are a liar. If you have transgressed all four of these commandments then you are a blasphemer, thief, fornicator and a liar. Do you think God will allow you into Heaven? What kind of place would Heaven be if God allowed blasphemers, thieves, fornicators and liars into it. I'll tell you, it wouldn't be a Holy place, and it wouldn't be Heaven.

With just four out of ten commandments we have had a glimpse of holiness. The Bible states, Wherefore the law *is* holy, and the commandment holy, and just, and good. "...but I am carnal, sold under sin." (Rom. 7:12,14)

The truth of the matter is that you are not holy, nor are you even good, and neither am I. We all are sinners and have broken His commandments.

> The Bible says, 1Cor. 6:9 Know ye not that the unrighteous shall not inherit the kingdom of God? Be not deceived: neither fornicators, nor idolaters, nor adulterers,

nor effeminate, nor abusers of themselves with mankind, 10 Nor thieves, nor covetous, nor drunkards, nor revilers, nor extortioners, shall inherit the kingdom of God.

Rev. 21:8 But the fearful, and unbelieving, and the abominable, and murderers, and whoremongers, and sorcerers, and idolaters, and all liars, shall have their part in the lake which burneth with fire and brimstone: which is the second death. Rev. 20:14 And death and hell were cast into the lake of fire. This is the second death. 15 And whosoever was not found written in the book of life was cast into the lake of fire.

If you die right now, according to the word of God, where will you go? Have you ever told a lie? Then you are a liar and according to the Bible you will go to the lake of fire. Is that where you want to go when you die? If you are in your right mind then you do not want to end up in the lake of fire for all eternity.

Is there a way to be saved from going to Hell? If you have been honest with yourself about those four commandments, then you know that you have broken at least one of them. The Bible says, For whosoever shall keep the whole law, and yet offend in one *point*, he is guilty of all. (James 2:10) Then according to the word of God you are guilty of breaking God's law and thus unable of your

Salvation

own self to enter Heaven.

In your present condition you will one day stand before your Creator and Judge who will pronounce the judgement; *"Guilty!"* The punishment for you is that you will be cast into Hell and then later cast into the lake of fire. That is what you deserve, and that is what I deserve as well, but this is where the good news begins.

Jesus Christ was God manifest in the flesh. That means Jesus Christ was fully God. He came to this earth, born of the virgin Mary, and became a man. While on this earth He never broke God's law one time. Jesus Christ lived a perfect life according to His law. Jesus Christ is Holy.

How do I know this? Because after He was crucified on the cross, our Lord arose from the dead after spending three days and three nights in the heart of the earth. If Jesus Christ had sinned one time, then He never would have been able to rise from the dead. He would have been just like you and me. But He did rise from the dead and was seen by over 500 people after He arose from the dead.

Jesus Christ saw you long before you were ever around. He saw you and He loved you.

> For God so loved the world, that he gave his only begotten Son, that whosoever believeth in him should not perish, but have everlasting life. John 3:16

God gave his Son; how? He gave him when

Jesus died on the cross as a sacrifice for our sins. Jesus Christ took the punishment of our sins upon Himself, and shed His blood as the perfect payment for your sins. The sins that you committed when you transgressed those commandments have all been paid for.

> Rom. 5:6 For when we were yet without strength, in due time Christ died for the ungodly. 7 For scarcely for a righteous man will one die: yet peradventure for a good man some would even dare to die. 8 But God commendeth his love toward us, in that, while we were yet sinners, Christ died for us. 9 Much more then, being now justified by his blood, we shall be saved from wrath through him.

While you were a sinner, Jesus Christ loved you and died for you on the cross. He also shed His blood as the payment for your sins, but you must pick up the payment. Rom. 6:23 For the wages of sin *is* death; but the gift of God *is* eternal life through Jesus Christ our Lord. Wages are given as payment for something that you have worked for. Those commandments that you have broken have earned you death. That is your payment, that is what you have worked for.

A gift is something that you do not work for. A gift is given free of charge after the giver worked to purchase it, or to make it. The gift that I am writing about here is eternal life. Do you want to live forever? Do you want to go to Heaven when

Salvation

you die? It is a free gift, but there is one catch. You must receive the Lord Jesus Christ in order to obtain eternal life.

Eternal life is not obtained through baptism, church membership, getting rid of bad Karma, or any other works. It is obtained through our Lord Jesus Christ. He is the One that paid the price. You must receive Jesus Christ as your very own personal Saviour.

> John 1:10 He was in the world, and the world was made by him, and the world knew him not. 11 He came unto his own, and his own received him not. 12 But as many as received him, to them gave he power to become the sons of God, *even* to them that believe on his name: 13 Which were born, not of blood, nor of the will of the flesh, nor of the will of man, but of God.

So how do you receive Jesus Christ? If you can't see Him, feel Him or touch Him, how can you receive Him? Rom. 10:13 For whosoever shall call upon the name of the Lord shall be saved. You must pray and ask Jesus Christ to forgive you of your sins; to wash you from your sins in His own blood; and ask Him to come into your heart and save you *from your sins*. Rev. 1:5 And from Jesus Christ, *who* is the faithful witness, *and* the first begotten of the dead, and the prince of the kings of the earth. Unto him that loved us, and washed us from our sins in his own blood.

Summary:
1. You have broken God's Holy Commands. Blasphemer, Thief, Fornicator or Liar - Guilty! Headed for the Lake of fire.

2. Jesus Christ died for your sins, was buried and three days later arose from the grave proving that He was God manifest in the flesh. He paid for all of your sins. Your ticket to Heaven is all paid for, now you must receive Jesus Christ into your heart in order to claim the payment for your sins.

3. You must call upon the Lord Jesus Christ to forgive you of your sins, to wash you in His blood, and ask the Lord Jesus Christ to come into your heart and save you.

Here is a simple prayer to pray. Remember though, that by faith in what God said, you are talking to Jesus Christ from your heart. Reciting this prayer will not save you. You must realize that you are talking to your Saviour, Jesus Christ. He is the One you need to forgive you and to save you. He promised to save you if you called and God cannot lie. The best way you know how pray this prayer out loud. Talk to the Lord out loud.

Dear Lord Jesus Christ. I come to you as a sinner who has broken your commandments. I am

Salvation

guilty. I believe you died on the cross and paid for my sins. Please forgive me of my sins. Please wash me throughly in your blood. And dear Jesus, please come into my heart and save me, I don't want to go to the lake of fire. Thank you for dying for me on the cross and thank you for saving me. In your name Lord Jesus I ask these things, Amen.

If you prayed a prayer like that one and meant it then according to the word of God I ask you, "Where are you now going when you die?"

Rom. 10:13 For whosoever shall call upon the name of the Lord shall be saved. That is a promise from God.

John 6:37 All that the Father giveth me shall come to me; and him that cometh to me I will in no wise cast out.

Dealing With Bad In-Laws

Other Works by Ken McDonald:

Here Comes The Bride:
A critique of the Baptist Bride heresy.
Is the true local Baptist church the bride of Jesus Christ? I extensively quote from their materials and then show from the word of God where they are wrong.

Pursuit:
One man's quest to find God's will for his life.
This book is a very transparent and personal testimony of the years I spent trying to find God's perfect will for my life.

Defiled:
The spiritual dangers of alternative medicine.
What does the word of God have to say about Alternative medicine?

Jesus Talk to me:
Have you ever wanted to get God's attention?
Why God pays attention to some and ignores others.

Even As God:
Healing relationships biblically
From being trespassed against to reconciliation, this book covers the steps of how God forgives, and according to Scripture is our pattern to follow.

Salvation

www.ingramcontent.com/pod-product-compliance
Lightning Source LLC
Chambersburg PA
CBHW052027290426
44112CB00014B/2413